Raeside's Canada

From Antigonish
to
Zebra Mussels

Also by Adrian Raeside:

There Goes the Neighbourhood:
An Irreverent History of Canada

The Demented Decade:
The Mulroney Years, What Really Happened

Dennis the Dragon
(with Joan Raeside)

Forthcoming (maybe):

The Novels of Fyodor Dostoevsky: A Jungian Approach

The Collected Wit of "Canada AM"

Raeside's Canada

From Antigonish
to
Zebra Mussels

ADRIAN RAESIDE

Doubleday Canada Limited

Canadian Cataloguing in Publication Data

Raeside, Adrian, 1957–
        Raeside's Canada

ISBN 0-385-25476-9

1. Canada – Social life and customs – Caricatures and cartoons.
2. National characteristics, Canadian – Caricatures and cartoons.
3. Canadian wit and humor, Pictorial. I. Title.

NC1449.R34A4 1994 971'00207 C94-931107-3

Text design by David Montle
Printed and bound in Canada

Published in Canada by
Doubleday Canada Limited
105 Bond Street
Toronto, Ontario
M5B 1Y3

Acknowledgements

The author would like to thank the following: Captain Krayden and Lieutenant Laviolette of the Canadian Armed forces, who allowed me to go where no cartoonist has gone before; the crew of the Snowbirds who almost (but not quite) gave me a heart attack; Delta hotels, an oasis of sanity in an insane travel schedule; the MacDonald clan, who showed me what life is all about in the Maritimes, my editor, Christine Harrison, who took a meaningless jumble of pictures and words and made them into a book and my editor at the Times–Colonist, Don Vipond, who allowed me to go AWOL to finish this book.

Contents

Introduction

WE ARE CANADA BECAUSE EVERY OTHER COUNTRY ISN'T.

When I undertook to do this book with Doubleday, I had every confidence that I would be able to produce a book that would for once and for all define Canada.

I failed.

There is no one thing that defines this country. What makes Canada are ten unique provinces, two territories, thousands of individual towns, millions of fascinating people and more languages than you can shake a stick at.

Even though we take in immigrants from all over and accept them for who they are and allow them the freedom to keep their own language and citizenship, nine times out of ten these newcomers will be lined up outside the citizenship court the first day they're eligible. Canada has that effect on everyone. We all want to be part of Canada. Because we all make up Canada.

The only people who aren't a part of Canada are bank executives and Revenue Canada investigators. They're actually from another planet.

The following is my take on this country and the people who remain indefinable, mysterious, and (thank God) completely unique.

Antigonish

Canadians have a bit of a reputation for being reserved. Except in the Maritimes, where they are anything *but*. A Maritimer will talk your ear off at the drop of a sou'wester. Family ties are close on the East coast, with families taking their ancestry seriously. Any Maritimer can tell you exactly who his great great grandfather was, where he came from (probably Scotland) and what he had for dinner on August 1, 1764.

Although any bar anywhere in Canada will contain an ex-pat Maritimer, most Maritimers stick close to home, leaving only to pursue work. In Antigonish, Nova Scotia, most of the town are MacDonalds, which makes taking the school roll call a nightmare for the teacher, but makes the local sign painter's life an easy one.

Those who can't trace their Maritime roots back a hundred years or so are known as CFAs (Come from Aways). No word yet on what the Micmac Indians called the first settlers....

Then there are the Acadians, but that's another story (see *There Goes the Neighbourhood*). . . .

Across the Map in Eighty Words

DRIVING MISS VICTORIA:

Driving in Victoria is an exercise in restraint. DON'T be in a hurry to get anywhere, as you will only end up in hospital with burst blood vessels:

2:05 Remove a couple of parking tickets from windshield.
(Victoria has more parking commissionaires than policemen.)

2:08 Beat off Parking Commissionaire who is trying to write you yet another ticket.

2:12 Start engine, put on your indicator and wait for the traffic to allow you to pull out.

2:37 Pull out.

2:38 Get stuck behind a quaint double-decker tour bus belching clouds of evil-smelling black smoke and running at top speed (25kmh). In any other city, the inspector of motor vehicles would have condemned these buses years ago, but this is Victoria and tourism is sacred.

2:39 It's either roll the windows down, breathe in bus exhaust and shorten your life, or roll the windows up and die of heat stroke/suffocation. You roll the windows up.

2:42 Just as the temperature in the car is topping 180 degrees, you spot a place to pass the bus and do so at mach 10.

2:43   You are past the bus and are thrilled to get the car out of first gear for the first time in two weeks.

2:44   Get stuck behind a 1954 Morris Oxford driven by a seventy-eight-year-old lady on the way to the Foul Bay liquor store–at 15 kmh.

2:47   You are now going so slow that pedestrians are passing you. Blood vessels on your head are starting to bulge and throb.   You grind another 1/8" off your teeth.

2:54   You turn a corner and run straight into the back of a Tally Ho (whoever thought of that name should be shot) tour coach, pulled by two bored-looking horses.   A bus load of tourists from Iowa are being subjected to a running commentary over the coach's P.A. system which is cranked up loud enough for benefit of elderly, hard-of-hearing patrons, as well as elderly, hard-of-hearing neighbours.

3:03 YES! A passing space is coming up, you put on your indicator and begin to pull out. Unfortunately, the six cretins on rental scooters who came up behind you a couple of minutes ago pull out and pass you instead. (Why is it that the size and weight of tourists who rent those abominable scooters is in inverse proportion to the size and weight of the scooters?)

3:10 You have passed the Tally Ho coach and are now cruising unimpeded through the James Bay district of Victoria. You are keeping a keen eye out, you know they are out there, just waiting to leap out at you.

3:15 You park the car and step out into a large fresh pile of steaming horse droppings. You use the back bumper of the next car to clean off your shoe and walk off down the street smelling of...Victoria.

3:16 A parking commissionaire pounces on your car. You forgot to plug the meter.

VANCOUVER

Ever since Expo '86 Vancouverites have been basking in the glow of billions of Hong Kong dollars. This hasn't come without a price. Shaunnessey–one of the more exclusive areas in Vancouver and once prime minister *du jour* John Turner's riding (not that anyone ever saw him there)–has been transformed into a ghetto of "monster houses." The Taiwanese and Hong Kong Chinese have been knocking down elegant old three-storey homes and putting up sprawling monstrosities. Now the good white folk feel just like the Indians did two hundred years ago, when the white settlers knocked down the stately old fir trees and started "civilizing" the country.

THE TRUE NORTH

Like Peter Mansbridge's forehead, Canada's North appears to be a vast wasteland. Unlike Peter Mansbridge's forehead, it isn't.

Nothing is more identifiably Canadian than our Far North—the Arctic. Northern Canada is defined as whatever isn't huddled along-side the U.S. border, as far south as we can get without needing a green card.

Canadians as a whole are largely ignorant of our Northern regions. Dog sleds, polar bear hunts, igloos and the now retired DEW line spring to mind. We tend to romanticize the Arctic and think of it as a pristine wilderness that will look after itself.

If we didn't have a federal government and the automobile hadn't been invented, the Arctic would probably still be that way—pristine. What the oil companies haven't dug up the Feds have screwed up. The relocation of the Inuit was one of the more infamous screw ups. Training NATO fighter pilots at 15 feet above the caribou herds was another. All in all, there aren't too many reasons for Northern residents to erect statues of Ottawa politicians.

The Arctic is, in fact, the most fragile part of Canada (if you discount the egos on Parliament Hill). The growing season is shorter than an average Italian government's term. What does grow is delicate and vitally important to the local fauna foraging for breakfast on a frigid winter morning. Survival of the flora and fauna is, in turn, vital to the survival of the natives, who have been living off the land for thousands of years before Greenpeace and the politically correct showed up.

And just because the Natives can endure minus 50 degree weather doesn't mean they're able to withstand cheap booze, crappy television and bureaucrats from Ottawa. If Churchill, Manitoba had palm trees and a five-star hotel, maybe our elected representatives and electronic media might go up more often and actually include the North in the decision-making process. Perhaps if Canada's two airlines reduced the fares to the North more Canadians might consider taking their holidays there instead of Florida or Hawaii.

Southern Canada telling Northerners how to run their lives is like Ottawa telling the rest of the country how to save money.

THE PRAIRIES

—

If there is a Hell, I hope they are readying a special spot for those who started the latest social leprosy currently sweeping the country: line dancing.

It is doubtful any of these establishments' patrons even knows what a cow looks like, but every Friday night, these party-goers race home to tear off their wool suits and button up embroidered shirts ($195), squeeze into their three-sizes-too-small jeans ($150), pull on hand-tooled cowboy boots ($800) and high tail it to Hank's.

Alberta is home to numerous watering holes that are country bars mainly because they *are* in the country. In Edmonton and Calgary, there is a heavy concentration of *urban* country bars, all offering line dancing lessons. As asinine as the jitterbug and as boring as watching the Commons pass a bill, line dancing has swept across the prairies and now has spread to other Canadian cities from Victoria to Saint John's.

The Prairies are the heart of Canada. Like arteries, railroad lines pump millions of bushels of grain to Canadian ports for export all over the world. From produce to beef, Canada's farms raise the best. Farming is clearly one of Canada's most important assets, but it's also the section of our economy that is most taken for granted.

If farmers finally walked away from agricultural delights such as: hail, locusts, crop disease, drought, bankers, floods, frost, federal reg-ulations, rail strikes, longshoremen's strikes and blistered hands, the entire country would starve.

TORONTO

—

What happened to Toronto? T.O. was once one of the most livable cities in North America. A place where drunks and women (and drunken women) could roam the streets freely at 2 a.m. without fear of being mugged–or worse. Toronto is now teeming with crack dealers, homeless people, coke-crazed pimps and urban planners.

There are numerous theories as to why Canada's largest city hit the skids: recession, immigration, cancellation of "The Journal," the election of the NDP.... Yonge Street, Toronto's main drag, has now become literally that, with drag queens blending with the endless tide of homeless, insane, and hopeless who daily struggle up Canada's busiest street. Yonge Street has not yet become a combat zone like Detroit's inner city but Toronto city council would rather collectively immolate themselves than confront the growing problems on the street.

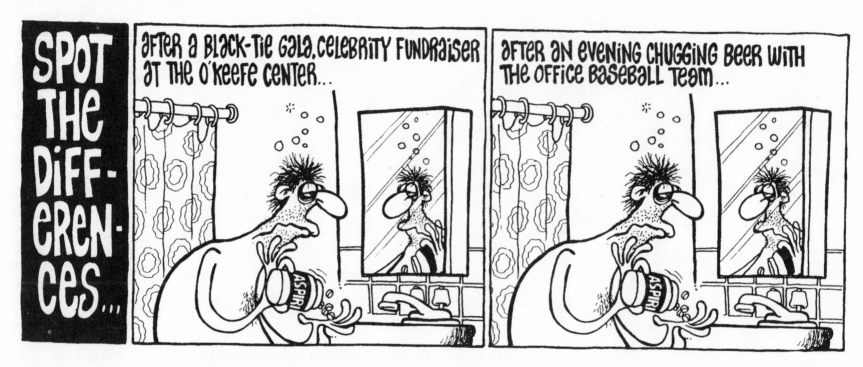

Toronto has for years boasted it is a world-class city. Now it has world-class problems. This, however, has done wonders for the morale of the rest of Canada, who has long suffered Toronto's superiority complex. Toronto is the city that everyone loves to hate.

WHY THE REST OF CANADA HATES TORONTO:

IT HAS A SUBWAY THAT ACTUALLY WORKS AND EVEN GOES SOMEWHERE.
(Unlike Vancouver's and Calgary's that go nowhere.)

MOST OF THE MAJOR BANKS ARE HEADQUARTERED IN TORONTO. (Say no more.)

ROY THOMSON HALL AND THE SKYDOME
Roy Thomson Hall is pretty exciting if all you have near you is the Elks Lodge. But take heart. Winnipeg's fabulous ballet, Quebec's Celine Dion, Alberta's k.d. lang, Nova Scotia's Rita MacNeil and Vancouver's Bryan Adams have all played Toronto. Toronto supplies the venue, the rest of Canada supplies the talent.

THE BLUE JAYS
O.K. O.K. The Jays are definitely the winningest team in North America and have beaten the U.S. at its own game–twice.

OTTAWA

The best roads and cleanest sidewalks in Canada have to be in Ottawa. The National Capital Commission that oversees all construction and maintenance in Ottawa has a seemingly unlimited budget. There *are* holes in the roads in Ottawa. But those are manmade and usually dug at around 6:30 a.m. outside your hotel room. I assume they are dug by the Receiver General to hide the millions of tax dollars that arrive in the capital daily.

Like a show Pomeranian, Ottawa is preened, shampooed and put on show for foreign diplomats and mere mortal shleps from the rest of the country who can scrape up the airfare to make the pilgrimage. Judging by the traffic that chokes Ottawa's streets at any one time, there are thousands of tourists driving aimlessly around in homage to the monuments of excess.

Because of Ottawa's proximity to the more enlightened Hull–just across the river but, culturally, light years away–most of the grey-flannel army live in Hull and commute to Ottawa. That would probably explain the ratio of one bus for every five people. If you enjoy standing on the sidewalk, thrilling as a number 57 majestically rolls past you, the ground shaking, the exhaust proudly pouring forth, set- ting your nostrils quivering as you take in a lungful of diesel, Ottawa's the place for you.

QUEBEC

—

Despite what separatists might tell you, Quebec always has been and always will be part of Canada. Quebec gives Canada that much needed *joie de vivre*. If it wasn't for the ridiculously high cost of air travel and nearly non-existent train service within the country, more Canadians outside *la belle province* would be able to experience Quebec.

Driving from Ottawa to Hull is like going to another country, except the Canadian dollar is accepted at par. The food is different, the language is different, the music is different, the pace of life is different. As you move deeper into darkest Quebec, the food gets better and more French is spoken. (Or less English, depending on how you view bilingualism.)

Bilingualism. Once the hot topic at any cocktail party or dinner table, the subject has now been accepted as reality. It does have its positive side. Think how many Canadians have learned French just by staring at their Rice Krispies box every morning. That's how we

learn our other official language in Canada—by osmosis. There still are local councils in small towns that will from time to time declare themselves English only, in protest against federal fiscal favouritism towards Quebec. This is unlikely to unravel Canada's social fabric, but it could prove a nuisance if an anglophone had to dispute a parking ticket in French.

Politicians both in Quebec and the rest of Canada have taken to declaring that Quebec is a "distinct society." They are, of course, absolutely right. The owner of the bakery who bakes mouth-watering *baguettes* is distinct. So is the Newfoundland fisherman who brings in lobsters, so is the Saskatchewan wheat farmer, so is the B.C. logger. Canada as a whole is distinct and Canadians get along just fine together. It's the politicians who can't get along with each other.

Quebec shouldn't separate from Canada. Canada should separate from Ottawa.

THE MARITIMES

Economically, Prince Edward Island is in a similar position as the other maritime provinces, with one exception: Anne of Green Gables, Inc. Lucy Maud Montgomery had no idea when she dusted off the old Olivetti and pounded out the first Anne book that she would eventually end up supporting an entire province. The only place in Canada that you will see more Japanese tourists is Whistler, B.C.

The tourist brochures marvel over the rolling fields of red clay. There *is* red clay, but it's likely to be covered over with a mini-golf establishment or an amusement park/shopping mall. One mall even features a fibreglass replica of the space shuttle.

The rest of Canada has great fun at the expense of all Maritimers. Newfie jokes are part of our cultural heritage. Maritimers tend to have large families, many of whom leave to find work elsewhere in Canada. Most of this mirth portrays the Maritimers navigating the urban ghettos in central Canada as halfwits. If being a halfwit means that you can endure hopeless unemployment, keep the family unit intact despite grinding poverty and still keep your sanity and a sense of humour, then I personally would be proud to be called a halfwit. (*Pleased to oblige*, ed.)

But like the Energizer bunny, the Maritimes just keep going and going and going. . . . It's unfair that such a beautiful part of Canada should be relegated to the back of Ottawa's priority bus. Maybe the Nova Scotia government should charge a toll to drive the Cabot Trail, say, $2.00 per car– $200 if you're from Ottawa.

In the Maritimes you can peer into Canada's past and see the resilient pioneer spirit that we once had. Maybe Maritimers could charge an admission fee like you pay at a museum, say, $2.00 per head– $200 if you're from . . .

Air Travel: Up Where the Food is Bad

Once upon a time, there were three airlines in Canada and flying was a reasonably pleasurable experience. Now, after the demise of Wardair and CP having been swallowed up by Pacific Western (like a guppy swallowing a whale) with the ensuing sniping and whining for government handouts, getting on a plane in Canada is similar to the thrill one would get from being herded onto a cattle car–without the amenities of the cattle car. There are always a few charter airlines that operate on the fringes, but their mandate is to pack as many people onto a plane as possible (see diagram).

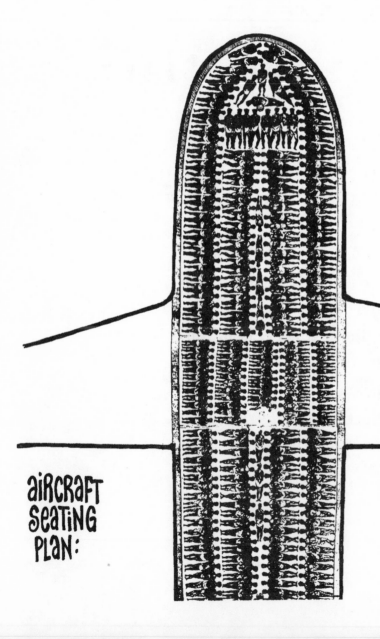

aiRCRAFT
SeaTiNG
PLaN:

Is it any wonder that Canada is unable to come together as a unified country, when flying from Vancouver to visit your old Aunt Dolly in Halifax is twice as expensive as a trip to London, England, two shows, hotel for a week, a couple of hookers, breakfast and airport transfers? There *are* occasional seat sales, but by the time you hear about them the handful of seats are long gone and you are forced to pay one of the bewildering array of exorbitant fares.

In early 1993, Canadian Airlines, née Wardair, née Canadian Pacific, held its breath until the taxpayer coughed up $50 million to keep it flying. Meanwhile, across town, Al's Widget Inc. was going out of business because they had the misfortune to shell out their own hard-earned dollars to upgrade equipment and remain competitive in the marketplace. Their market shrank and free trade allowed U.S. manufacturers using slave labour in Mexico to export into Canada at ridiculously low prices. Like so many others, Al went out of business without receiving a penny from the federal (*that's enough,* ed.)

Canadian survived, Air Canada dropped its lawsuit and they both went back to doing what they do best–nothing.

MOST ASKED QUESTIONS WHEN ON A CANADIAN AIRLINE:

- Why does this steak have "Nike" written on it?

- Why is it cabin attendants are suddenly deaf when you press the call button?

- Why was the baby with colic and an ear infection put in the next seat? In business class...

- What is that green speckly stuff next to the salad and has it ever been near Chernobyl?

- Is the dessert part of some scientific experiment?

- Why is this non-stop flight stopping in Winnipeg?

- Does the airline *really* pay someone to go into the plane and break the back of each seat before every flight?

- Why does the captain choose to get on the loudspeaker in the middle of the only snooze you were getting? (Who cares whether Moose Jaw is on the right side or the left side of the plane? How much are you going to see from five miles up anyway?)

If the airlines were at all smart, they'd bring back the free booze. Get us all whizzed so we forget that the seat back is broken, the "food" is rancid and the "food" tray has collapsed.

MULTI-COLOURED
PCB JELLY

SHREDDED
VINYL

ROAD KILL

OVERPRICED
PLONK

LUKE-WARM
SLUDGE

Art, Eh?

Canadians are desperate for our own cultural identity. So desperate in fact, that institutions like the National Galley in Ottawa scour the world looking for things we can hang on the wall and call our own. (See also Garage Sales.)

Case in point: "Voice of Fire" and "Number 16," both by American painters. The New York auction houses couldn't believe their luck when our Canadian cultural kamikazes descended on the art scene with bulging cheque books and empty heads and scooped up "Voice of Fire" (a red stripe on a blue background) for a measly $3.5 million. The gallery was chagrined at the derision from taxpayers when the work was finally hung in Ottawa. Determined to educate the non-believing philistines, they went on another raid of the

New York auction houses, returning with "Number 16" (a blank canvas surrounded by a square and a half) by Rothko for $1.6 million. (One should be thankful that Rothko's previous fifteen brilliant attempts were not available at the same time.)

"Number 16" was greeted with the same enthusiasm as "Voice of Fire" – though a handful of art critics did go on record extolling the wisdom of acquiring such a treasure for Canada. An art critic for the Montreal *Gazette* wrote a column blasting the barbarians who didn't appreciate the importance of such a brilliant work as "Number 16." To underscore her point, a photo of the painting was run at the end of her column. The next day, the *Gazette* ran an apology: "The *Gazette* regrets that due to a production error, 'Number 16' was printed upside down."

Say goodnight Gracie.

Canadians are prepared to spend millions of dollars soaking up American culture, which consists mainly of television programs geared for retarded oysters. Why we fawn over American artists and entertainers when Canada has more artists per capita than any other country in the world, remains a mystery. Maybe it's because we create for creation's sake. Americans have turned creation into a high-volume, hyped industry. Hollywood makes more money than all the gambling in the U.S. combined. Canadian artists are in many cases self-taught and live hand-to-mouth. It isn't that they enjoy that lifestyle; being an artist in a country so close to the U.S. is like trying to play the flute next to a heavy-metal rock band.

It's sad to think that 2,000 years from now, when what is left of Canada is being dug up by archaeologists from planet Zog, we shall be remembered by cultural gems like "Jeopardy" or "Rescue 911." We'll let the cockroaches explain away that one.

Canada is rich in Native art and folk art. I define Native art as any-thing created out of local materials by someone of indigenous descent. This craft and knowledge has usually been handed down over the centuries.

Folk art–to me–is anything created by someone who immigrat-ed to this country and has endured long winters inside with nothing but a couple of cords of wood and an axe. What they didn't burn for heat emerged as honest pieces of art, created strictly for their own enjoyment. Folk art is now a thriving industry in New York, the· original pieces long ago absorbed into the darkness of private collec-tions. What is being turned out now is probably produced in a fac-tory in China, with Black & Decker routers and chainsaws. But it is still possible to pick up the odd piece of genuine folk art in Canada, the Maritimes being your best bet. Buy from the artist. You know what you're getting and he/she isn't being screwed by a gallery. WARNING: A bad French accent does not necessarily mean the artist is genuine, but it does make the transaction more entertaining.

In recent years, so-called Native art has been cranked out by white artists. Supposedly as a tribute to our heritage, to mix the mediums, keep the art alive, blah blah blah…It is really just a blatant attempt by white carvers and artists to cash in on the resurgence of interest in Native culture. To call what these white forgers are producing traditional Native art is like comparing Mayan pottery with Tupperware.

Native art was originally intended to preserve legends and tribal history. The heraldic symbols on the carvings bridged the worlds of men and animals and were important ceremonial tools. It was their version of our encyclopedia. Along came the white man. We took their land, took their pride and took their lives. Now we've come back for their culture.

One wonders at the reaction of the arts community if Willy Joe in the Cold Lake Reserve spent a few minutes with a can of red paint and a paint roller and produced a painting he called "Number 17."

It's a safe bet that he would not get $1.6 million and that the painting would not hang in the National Gallery.

Greedy, Avaricious, Dishonest, Usurious, Callous, Lowlife, Imperious, Uncaring, Lying, Cold, Unfeeling, Sneaky Weasels

Yes, this is the section on Canadian Banks.

The Bank Charter

- **This bank is forbidden to provide a reasonable level of service.**

- **The bank is permitted—and encouraged—to charge whatever it likes for the aforementioned non-service.**

- **The bank will construct all buildings in such a way as to make each customer feel like an insignificant piece of (enough, ed.)...**

- **No more than two (2) wickets shall be open at peak periods.**

- **A minimum of three (3) errors will be required on any given bank statement.**

- **Unsecured loans to shifty international developers who eventually go bankrupt will be rewarded with layoffs at the teller level and promotions on the executive floor.**

Canadian banks spend millions of dollars insulting our intelligence with puerile television commercials showing happy, smiling customers hugging their bank manager in front of their newly-purchased home. In reality, Charlie Manson gets more respect than the average Canadian looking for a loan.

HOW TO GET A LOAN AT A CANADIAN BANK:

Step 1: Make an appointment with the receptionist at the bank "service counter" (one of the world's great oxymorons) to see a loans manager. These people usually exude the same warmth as a Revenue Canada investigator.

Step 2: Wait in the reception area surrounded by other sweating borrowers clutching bags containing financial statements, dog-eared payroll stubs and bags of Tums.

Step 3: Joy! Your name is called and you are ushered into the inner sanctum. Your heart rate goes up, your palms sweat, your bowels loosen. All you are looking to borrow is $11,500 for a second-hand car, but you get the feeling that you may as well ask for $11.5 million. The loans officer looks over your financial statements. He/she/it says nothing, but you watch, mesmerized, for any sign that your miserable worth will make their criteria.

Step 4: The interrogation: How long have you worked at your job? The job before that? Before that? Do you mind if we check? (They will.) Ever been turned down for a loan before? (This must be an intelligence test. Only a complete idiot would answer yes to that one.) What is the value of your household furniture? (Let's see...a couch you got from the Goodwill eight years ago, a bed given to you ten years ago–the stains on the mattress look like something recently purchased by the National Gallery–a coffee table with 2,571 cigarette burns in it, and a couple of posters of Jimi Hendrix. Total: $11,500.)

Step 5: The loans officer has everything needed to make the decision. You will be called tomorrow. You exit, feeling pretty good about how things went. Besides, you've been banking with them for 12 years, you have $4,000 in a savings account, $2,500 in RRSPs, a steady income of $28,000 per year and a good credit record.

Step 6: You're called by the loans officer. Your application has been denied.

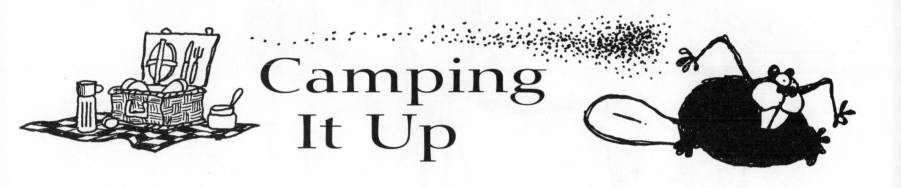

Camping It Up

Canadians love camping.

Judging by the disposable diapers secreted in the bushes around campgrounds, this passion starts early. What Canadian teenager hasn't had his/her first grope in a pup tent tucked in beside the latrines in a provincial park?...Besides being a training ground for procreation, parks also serve as clandestine beer parlours. Away from the prying eyes of parents, generations of teenagers have sampled the adult delights of drinking vodka, rye, gin and beer (all in the same glass and in the space of about 25 minutes), vomiting, then passing out on the grass.

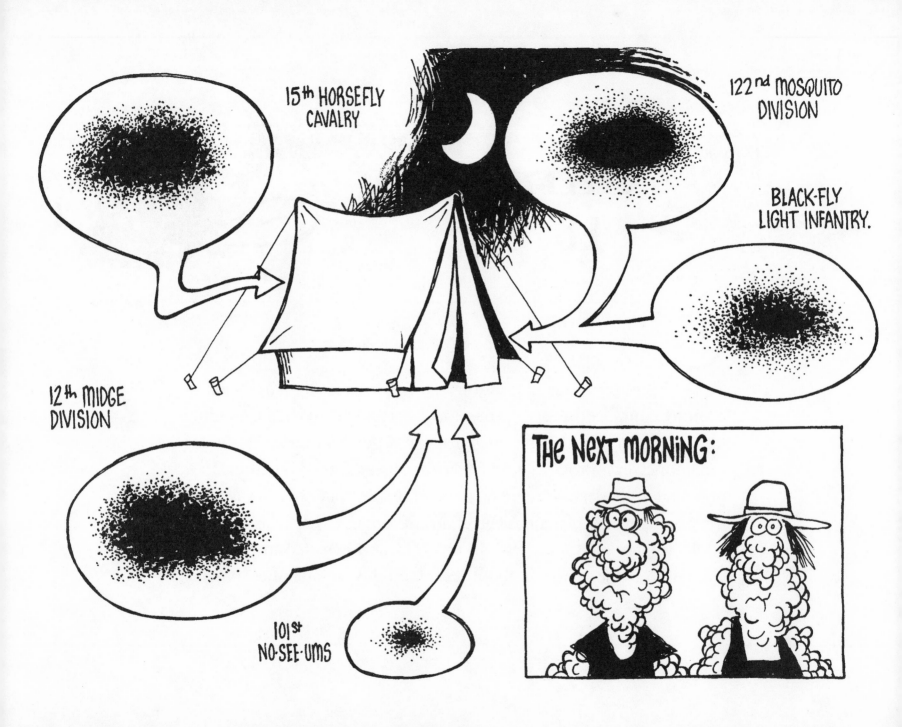

Unfortunately, there are also adults who wish to relive their youth by knocking back a couple of dozen cold ones in their campsite, then using the empty bottles as baseballs. These people are, of course, scum and should be forced to eat their debris.

Fortunately, these boors are in the minority; most Canadians are proud of their parks. City, municipal, provincial, federal–you can't travel more than a few kilometres before you'll come across a chunk of protected green space.

FIVE MOST IMPORTANT THINGS TO BRING ON A CAMPING TRIP:

1. Insect repellent

2. Insect repellent

3. Insect repellent

4. Insect repellent

5. Insect repellent

For those who love the outdoors, but consider the ultimate in roughing it to be a black-and-white TV with no remote control, there is the camper. From modest plywood barrios built on the back of an old Datsun pickup, to twenty metre air-conditioned behemoths, the wilderness can be less than a couple of hours away (depending on

traffic). What is incredible is not what creature comforts can be found in these campers, but how many people can fit in one. Haitian refugee boats are positively spacious compared to putting a family of six, two dogs, a cat and supplies for a week in a truck camper. God knows how many camping holidays have been catalysts for divorce.

A lot of camping vehicles never leave the pavement. Hopping from trailer park to trailer park, the closest they come to the wilderness is a *National Geographic* documentary via the trailer park's satellite hookup.

Gives the wildlife peace and quiet, anyway.

COTTAGE COUNTRY

Every Friday afternoon throughout those long, hot, humid Toronto summers, Torontonians flee the city out to the Muskokas or Georgian Bay. Perhaps more orderly than the exodus of Jews from Russia, but no less of a religious experience. In theory.

The only thing better than having a cottage in Ontario, is *knowing* someone who has a cottage. This eliminates the chore of opening and closing the cottage every spring and fall. Besides, you also don't worry about what to do with the mountain of empties and smouldering briquettes after a politically *incorrect* weekend.

Some cottages wouldn't be out of place in Rosedale or Westmount and others could easily get lost in a Rio slum. Yet the owners of cottages without electricity, television and running water are proud to claim that they are the only true cottagers. (But don't expect to see them *en residence* come playoff season....)

On the West coast, instead of cottages, they have chalets. On or near a ski hill and used mainly in the winter, these are usually in a condo/apartment complex, modern and *very* expensive. To pay the outrageous mortgages on these condos, they are usually put in a condo-management company and rented out. Whether you make your mortgage payment can depend on the amount of snow that year.

Deep Fried Snowbirds

Anyone who can, abandons central and eastern Canada for at least two weeks in the winter. The closest and most popular destination is Florida. Apparently, the prospect of being killed in a drive-by shooting or being robbed at knifepoint doesn't seem too bad compared with driving the 401 in a blizzard, during rush hour.

Ontarians and Quebecers pour into the Sunshine State by the 747-load every winter. Toronto males cavort about wearing fairly conservative bathing shorts, while Quebec males, anxious to expose as much of their skin as possible to melanoma, squeeze into teeny weeny Speedos. The overall effect is similar to stretching dental floss over a beetroot.

DAY 1 BEACHED BELUGA

DAY 2 PAR-BOILED

DAY 3 FRIED

DAY 4 CREMATED

Floridians complain that besides being fashionably inept, Canadians are financially myopic when it comes time to pay the bar tab. These Americans still haven't realized that Canada is a third-world country, whose currency is worthless south of the 49th parallel. There are Somalians and Ethiopians walking around the beaches with more money to burn than your average Snowbird.

The Environment: Hugging the Whales

Once, those who were concerned about the environment or those who chose to live off the land were considered "oddball, but quaint." The international environmental movement got its start in Canada in the 60s, as Canada was and still is tolerant of alternate thinking. (How many other countries declare senators a protected species?) As the baby boomers grew up, many began tiring of the succession of BMWs and Club Med holidays. An irrational desire to distance themselves from conspicuous consumption surfaced. The Greenpeace canvassers who for years had been walking the streets as enviro-bag ladies, found fistfuls of cash thrust upon them. Suddenly,

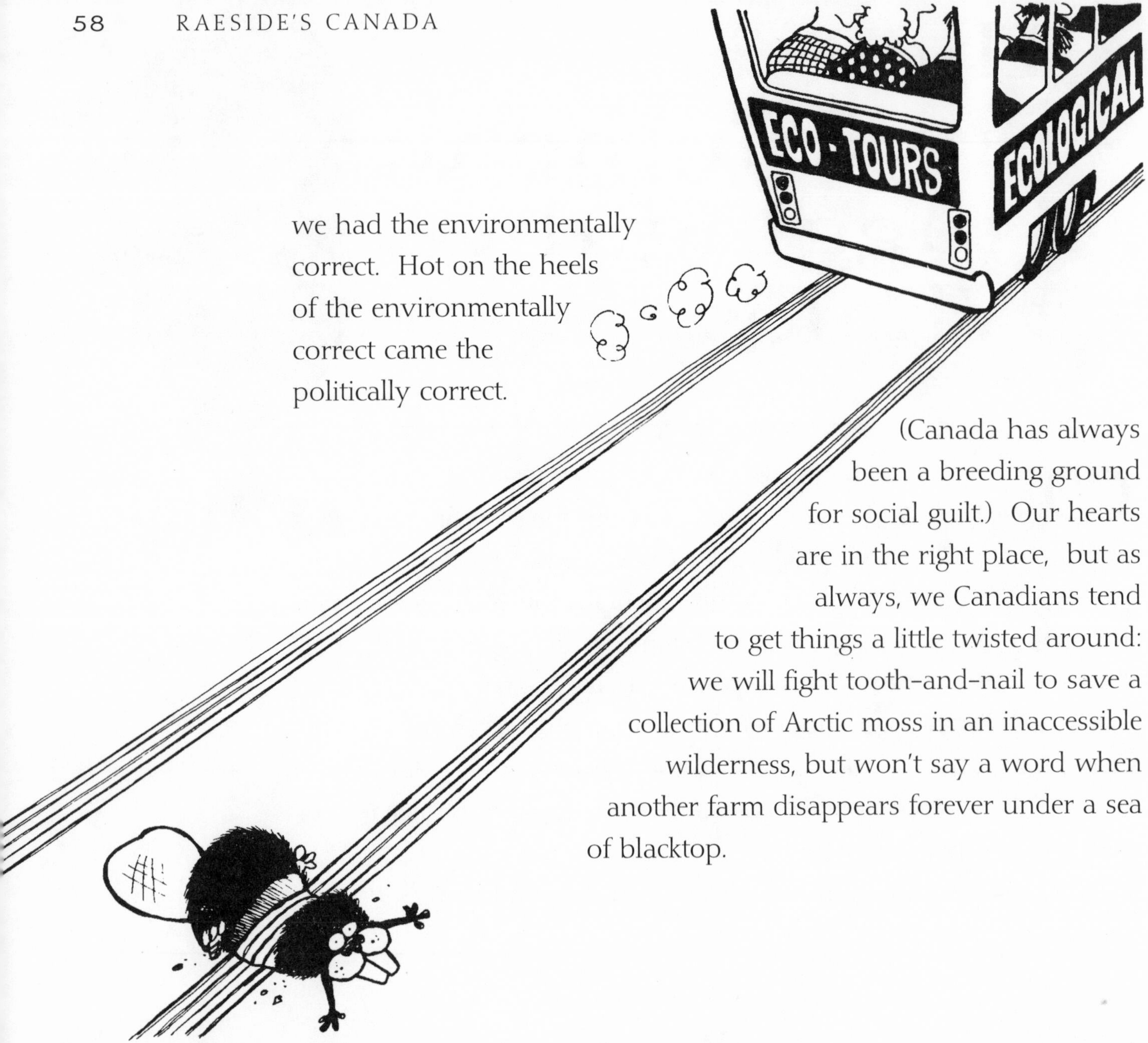

ECO - TOURS

ECOLOGICAL

we had the environmentally correct. Hot on the heels of the environmentally correct came the politically correct.

(Canada has always been a breeding ground for social guilt.) Our hearts are in the right place, but as always, we Canadians tend to get things a little twisted around: we will fight tooth-and-nail to save a collection of Arctic moss in an inaccessible wilderness, but won't say a word when another farm disappears forever under a sea of blacktop.

We will break the law to save the habitat of the Marbled Murrelet or the Spotted Owl. We will then go home and drench the garden in pesticide, eventually finishing off scores of sparrows, robins and finches.

We will protest the passage of supertankers down our coast, but will complain bitterly when the price of gas goes up two cents a litre.

STEPS TO TAKE TO BE COMPLETELY ENVIRONMENTALLY CORRECT:

1. Do not wear fur.
2. Do not wear leather. Start buying cardboard shoes.
3. Do not eat meat. It is laced with steroids.
4. Do not eat vegetables. They are loaded with pesticides.
5. DO not buy anything plastic.
6. Do not buy anything made of wood.
7. Do not use detergents.
8. Do not use aerosols.
9. Do not use anything with PCBs.
10. Do not use anything with urea foam.

This is all moot of course, since researchers have discovered that cockroach farts are depleting the earth's ozone at an alarming rate, meaning we will all die from ultra-violet poisoning long before we expire from DDT. So, cheer up!

CLAYOQUOT SOUND

—

The Sound is the site of one of Canada's last stands of first-growth timber. That is, timber that hasn't yet been turned into chopsticks and copies of the *National Enquirer*. Although Clayoquot Sound is publicly-owned land, multinational MacMillan Bloedel and a handful of smaller companies have had the timber cutting rights to this area for a long time and are just now turning their chainsaws to the more sensitive parts of the Sound.

Disagreements over the use of public forests are going on across Canada, pitting the tree huggers against the tree muggers. Clayoquot Sound has become a rallying point for the environmentalists across Canada and an Alamo for the logging companies who fear if they lose this battle, all their other timber rights will go the same way.

The first logging trucks that rolled into the Sound after July 1, 1993, were met by a crowd of protestors who blocked the only road access across the Kennedy Lake bridge. MacBlo got a court order barring the protestors from standing on the road.

The RCMP set up a special detachment to process the daily intake of protesters arrested at the bridge every morning. Just getting arrested wasn't as simple as bolting onto the road from the crowd gathered at either side. It was planned. Monday would be seniors' day, Tuesday would be children's day, Wednesday would be women's day, Thursday Hermaphrodites' day, and so on. If you wanted to be arrested, you put your name down on a list the day before. Only in Canada is anarchy planned.

By the time winter set in and the blockaders took down the peace camp, 850 people had been arrested. Most now have criminal records.

CLAYOQUOT QUOTES

—

"I PLAN ON GETTING
ARRESTED IN THE FALL."

–15-year old at the
peace camp

"LOGGERS PAY
YOUR PENSIONS!"

–MacBlo employee

"TAKE CARE OF MY SIGN!"

-Raging granny

"THAT COULD BE YOUR
MOTHER!"

-Protester to RCMP
officer arresting a
raging granny

TO TURN A 1,000-YEAR-OLD
TREE INTO WOOD OR PULP
IS IN INDESCRIBABLE BAD
TASTE."

-Jim Willer, 72, arrested
at Kennedy Bridge,
August 19, 1993

"I FOUGHT IN THE LAST WAR
TO PROTECT THE FUTURE
FOR OUR PEOPLE. TODAY, I'M
DOING THE SAME DAMN
THING."

-Senior citizen as he's
being led away to the
police bus

ATTENTION ARRESTEES!
YOUR WAIVERS HAVE BEEN
PHOTOCOPIED AND ARE
NOW ON THE GREEN BUS!
DO NOT FORGET TO PICK
YOURS UP!!!!

-Sign on the peace
camp notice board

HAVE YOU WASHED YOUR
HANDS LATELY?

-Sign in peace camp
kitchen

"IF YOU DON'T CRY WHEN
FLYING OVER VANCOUVER
ISLAND, THERE'S SOME-
THING SICK ABOUT YOU."

-Lummi Nation Chief,
Jewel James,
September 13, 1993

KILL A HIPPIE, SAVE YOUR
JOB. HUG A LOGGER, YOU'LL
NEVER GO BACK TO TREES.

-Graffiti on the
highway to Tofino

WIPE YOUR ASS WITH A
SPOTTED OWL.
EARTH FIRST! WE'LL LOG
ANOTHER PLANET LATER.

-Slogans on T-shirts
worn by some
MacBlo loggers.

Garage Sales

YOU PAID *WHAT* FOR THAT??

A descent into the seamy, lurid world of garage sales.

It's a bizarre Canadian ritual. All across the country, seemingly normal people will routinely get up at the crack of dawn each Saturday, eager to get the jump on fellow fetishists. Although most garage sales start at 9 a.m., the serious buyers will wait in their cars as early as 7 a.m., engines idling, hearts pounding, imagining the possibility of finding an A.Y. Jackson hidden behind a black velvet painting of Elvis (or, for some, *vice versa*).

Still others are sweating at the thought they may have picked the wrong sale to begin the day's outing, and may arrive just in time to see a fabulous yellow sofa and loveseat ($15.00) being toted out by their next door neighbour.

The strategic planning for the D-Day invasion was sloppy compared with the serious garage saleaholic's itinerary for a given Saturday morning....

THE TEN MOST DESIRED *OBJETS* AT ANY GARAGE SALE:

1. Wide-mouthed pickling jars

2. Framed photos of Niagara Falls in the summer

3. Framed photos of Niagara Falls in the winter

4. Fondue sets (missing one fork)

5. Jigsaw puzzles (minus a couple of sky bits)

6. Corroded bronze jewellery

7. Miscellaneous tools

8. Tatty children's clothes

9. Anything made by K-Tel

10. Framed photos of Niagara Falls in the fall

And now that you've acquired a houseful of useless garbage gleaned from garage sales, you can go ahead and have your own sale.

The Great Outdoors

There are two types of sports fishermen (*fisherpersons, surely,* ed.) Those who, a couple of times a year, dust off the tackle box, drag the boat out of the weeds behind the house and launch it at the nearest beach for a day of fishing, drinking beer and enjoying the water. (Actually catching a fish would be welcome, but secondary.)

In these environmentally enlightened times, catch-and-release is the thing to do....And God said to Adam, "Go forth, and take the birds from the air, the animals from the field and the fish from the stream— but you gotta put them all back again."

The other type of fisherman is the hard-core fanatic. These people don't have just boats, they have *fishing machines.* Costing close to what a four-bedroom house will set you back in Mississauga, these high-tech slaugh-terhouses are built to do only two things: get to where the fish are, fast and catch them, fast. These fishermen have surveil-lance technology that can detect a fish fart, tell them what depth it's at, how many pounds the fish weighs and what it last ate. About the only guesswork left for these guys is whether to drink lite or regular beer. The only difference between one of these boats and the weapons control centre of the *HMCS Vancouver*, is that there are fewer drink holders on the *Vancouver*.

As Canada's saltwater fish stocks are depleted, fishermen are becoming ruthless in their pursuit. This isn't exactly fair to the fish, who also have to contend with Korean driftnets, gillnetters, seine net-ters, trollers, Native fisheries, El Nino, toxic waste dumps and oil spills. Not to mention the decimation of the herring stocks and the supposed explosion in the seal population. According to commercial fishermen, one seal can kill more salmon in a day than an entire fishing fleet can haul out in a month. About the only thing the seals aren't accused of is being responsible for late UIC cheques.

There is yet a third group of fisherpersons in Canada: the hard-core purists who believe the only way to catch fish is the sporting way. They're called fly fishermen. In basements all over Canada, fly fishermen hunch over vices, (*vises, surely*, ed.) surrounded by boxes of mouldy feathers, tying different combinations of feathers and coloured thread onto fish hooks, creating what one assumes is an irresistible *hors d'oeuvre* for fussy trout. It probably would be simpler to hurl an entire chicken into the river and see which part the trout nibbled first.

RECIPE FOR THE PERFECT, DEADLY FISHING FLY:

1. TWO FEATHERS FROM A LEGHORN ROOSTER'S SCROTUM

2. A GREEN FEATHER FROM A KENYAN PHEASANT'S EYEBROW

3. A SEQUIN FROM ELVIS' JUMPSUIT

4. TWO NOSE HAIRS (YOUR OWN, NOT ELVIS')

5. A DROP OF ANTARCTIC MINK OIL

CANADA'S COMMERCIAL FISHERY—*ADIOS*

To be a Canadian commercial fisherman you need to be able to go out in any weather without getting seasick, endure wet clothes, put up with dodgy food and whine about how badly the Federal Fisheries Department treats you. The complaints are passed on from father to son, rather like a precious heirloom. Like fishing tales, they get more outrageous with each telling. There *are* legitimate complaints, the most obvious being foreign boats over-fishing in Canadian waters.

In the days when there were plenty of fish on both coasts, it was a free-for-all to get as much fish into the processing plants in as short a time possible. Twenty years ago, Lunenburg harbour in Nova Scotia was packed with fishing boats. There were more people on boats than there were in the town itself.

"THOSE PARKING COMMISSIONAIRES TREAT US LIKE SCUM."

"BUT WE ARE SCUM."

-Conversation overheard between two B.C. commercial fishermen

The collapse of the East coast fishery started in the mid 80s and ended with a complete closure in 1993. The Fisheries Department blamed the fishermen and the processors for taking advantage of an antiquated and unenforceable quota system. The fishermen blamed the Fisheries for setting up an antiquated and unenforceable quota system and not accounting for fish stocks. The processors blamed the Feds for an antiquated and unenforceable quota system, not accounting for fish stocks and allowing foreign vessels to poach off Canadian fish stocks, *ad nauseam*. The only thing they all agreed on is that there are no bottom fish left.

It won't be long before fish fingers will be displayed in the seafood section of supermarkets–next to the caviar.

WHEN YOU GO DOWN TO THE WOODS TODAY...

(Be sure to wear your Kevlar vest.)

What is it, in the age of the .98¢ per kilo hamburger meat, that drives men and the occasional woman to arm themselves with the latest in high-tech weaponry and blaze away at anything on four legs that can be cut up to fit into a stewpot, or mounted on the den wall? Just asking.

It's been a number of years since Canadian pioneers were forced to kill the local fauna just to survive another miserable season. (See the historical masterpiece, *There Goes The Neighbourhood*, Doubleday, for a more indepth look at Canada's history.) Since then, we have evolved (regressed?) to a bastardized form of the English hunt. (We are not, of course, as refined as the English, who prefer to gather as a group with other syphilitic, idle members of the aristocracy most of whom have never done anything more strenuous than pass the port.)

Canadians at least have the gallantry to give the quarry a sporting chance. Piling into a pickup and careening through the woods does take some energy. Opening those beer cans burns up calories galore. In more remote areas–those that have only scattered RCMP patrols–a simple drive down a quiet back road at dusk, drawing a bead on two glowing points of light in the bushes is crude, but effective.

Wild game is regulated by the provincial governments, who, we assume, inherited that right from Adam. The value of individual species of game is determined by a tag system. (*Toe tags, surely?* ed.) For example, a moose is worth more than a deer. A black bear is worth less than a grizzly bear. (Unless you are a German tourist on a pilgrimage to plug a black bear, in which case it will cost you thousands more than a resident for the tag, a few thousand for the airfare and another two grand for a guide. The guide is the guy who leads the hunter to the unsuspecting animal's back yard and directs the hail of lead at the unsuspecting fauna for him.) Baggage restrictions being what they are on commercial airlines, it would be difficult for the visiting Buffalo Bill to drag the entire carcass home to Berlin, so usually just the head makes the trip.

Bears, who had been enjoying a respite from trophy hunters since the Coldstream Guards' headgear changed from bearskin to fun fur, now find themselves in the unenviable position of being popular, not for what they are wearing, but for what's inside them.

Some Asians believe that ingesting bear "bits" will help the "performance of a certain part of their anatomy." This is, of course, a myth. You don't see too many male bears starring in hard-core porno movies. (*How would you know?*, ed.) Regardless, there is now a roaring underground trade in bear gallbladders, claws, and genitalia of assorted sizes.

The seasonal death toll isn't just confined to our four-legged friends. Every year there are a few dozen two-legged carcasses packed out of the woods, either mistaken for bull moose, or caught in the crossfire. These are always treated by the authorities as "hunting accidents." One wonders why the Mafia don't organize more hunting trips....

A side effect to this carnage is that the traditional hunters—wolves, cougars, and the like are beginning to outnumber their prey (caribou for instance). It panics provincial governments to see their lucrative tag revenues and tourist dollars being threatened, so controlled "culls" are organized for these out-of-control predators. The Northern wolf packs are a prime example. They have been shot at from helicopters, poisoned and trapped to keep their numbers down. Unfortunately, as caribou tastes great and looks fabulous on a wall, the caribou herds continue to be depleted faster than the wolves.

DEER ALEX TILLEY

I FEEL COMPELLED TO RITE TO YOU. TO COMMEND YOU ON YUR LINE OF CLOTHING. THE WALKING SHORTS WERE DELISHUS. BUT SLITELY DRY. THE MATCHING KHAKI SHIRT WAS ALSO QUITE PALATABLE, BUT I FOUND THE SEKRET POCKET A LITTLE CHEWY. MAY I SUGGEST INKLUDING KETCHUP IN WITH YOUR FALL LINES?

HIC

The culling will probably continue, until wolves start buying ground beef at the supermarket for .98¢ per kilo, or the UN negotiates a unilateral ceasefire.

Lights, Camera, Government Grant

Because Canada has no self-supporting Hollywood to finance film and television production, the Canadian industry has to turn with hand outstretched to the government. Almost every level of government has something to give away. At the top is federally funded Telefilm, which normally gives money to bad French-Canadian art movies shot in a Montreal warehouse. These productions almost never make it to theatres or television. And not just because anglophones can't understand them. Francophones can't understand them either. To correct this cultural imbalance, Telefilm is funding more projects in the West and many of those are not making it to theatres for the same sort of reasons.

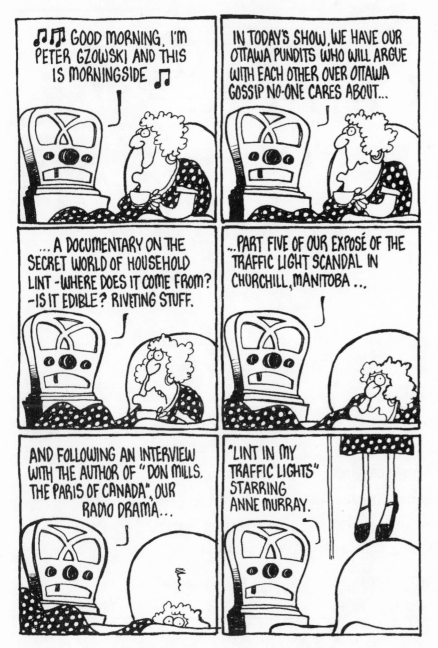

Local governments are a good hit for filmmakers. Wave a camera in front of a city councilman's face in any small town in Canada and the heavens will open up. Unfortunately, these golden geese have been visited once too often by dodgy movie producers who have skipped town leaving unpaid bills and shattered dreams of stardom.

One small town that had its brush with stardom is Nelson, B.C. Nelson was just a small, unpretentious interior town, until the cast and crew of *Roxanne* starring Steve Martin and Darryl Hannah turned up. Suddenly, Nelson was a STAR!

Half of Nelson was in the movie and the little town changed forever. Now, when you visit Nelson you can takethewalkingtourof*Roxanne*, seewhereSteveMartinstayed,seethefirehallinthemovie, seewhereDarrylHannahstayed, *ad nauseam*.

TV-wise, we *are* responsible for "The Beachcombers," "Road to Avonlea," and "W5." These are good shows and prove that Canadians can and do make good television. The CBC "Journal" was once great, but the CBC chief at the time killed it. And he didn't kill the CBC Nightly News, he just tortured it to death. Fecan should go on trial for treason.

It is curious how a network such as CBC Television, that receives government funding *and* sells commercial time should be in such constant financial difficulty, unlike CTV that manages to limp along, despite not being at the public trough and with their only revenue coming from selling commercials. Could it be that there are too many overpaid, no talent executives warming expensive leather recliners in the CBC headquarters in Toronto? Just asking.

For years, those who lived in the North had only one channel to watch–CBC. Fortunately, with satellite dishes becoming more affordable, there is more of a choice. Why watch "The Scarborough finals of Celebrity Mud Wrestlemania, hosted by Al Waxman," when you can watch "Celebrity Mud Wrestling, live from Boise, Idaho?

There are concerns that too much lousy American programming is being beamed across the border, rotting young Canadian minds. It is infinitely better than much of the mental dry rot being produced in Canada, by Canadians, for Canadians.

AN ALL-CANADIAN NIGHT OF TELEVISION:

6.00 p.m. LOCAL NEWS. Tonight: Beer smuggling between provinces, part 12 of a 100-part series on tax evasion and your guide to cross-border shopping. (1 hr.)

7.00 p.m. LEAVE IT TO BEAVER. Wally and the Beav come back from the U.S. with a car load of smokes, 4 litres of vodka and a couple of leather jackets. (30 min.)

7.30 p.m. ALL IN THE FAMILY. Archie hits the roof when his lesbian, crack-addicted, dropout daughter announces she is marrying a French-Canadian constitutional lawyer. (30 min.)

8.00 p.m. W5. A look at the banking system in Canada. (Parental discretion advised. (1 hr.)

9.00 p.m. Movie: THE BLACK HOLE. Two chums (Al Waxman, Bruno Gerussi) get jobs at Revenue Canada. Laughs galore, as these two wacky guys fumble from foreclosures to garnishées. (2 hrs.)

11.00 p.m. FRONT PAGE CHALLENGE. Four obscure Canadians try to guess the identity of a guest who no one has heard of or cares about. (30 min.)

11.30 p.m. LATE-NIGHT LOCAL NEWS. Beer smuggling between provinces, part 12 of a 100-part series on tax evasion and your guide to cross-border shopping. (30 min.)

12 midnight SPECIAL: The Constitution. What does it mean to Canadians? (8 hrs.)

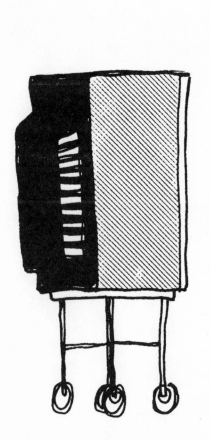

Lottery Fever

Canadians have a reputation for fiscal conversatism and are not easily parted from their money. The only exception is the lottery. Bar pull-tabs, Scratch 'n' Win, hockey pools, 6/49, it doesn't matter what it is, Canadians will happily drop a couple of bucks on the chance of winning anything from $2 to $2 million. When the 6/49 jackpot climbs over $5 million, Canadians go into a feeding frenzy of piranha-like proportions. Normally rational people will happily wait in line at the lottery counter to fork over their hard-earned dollars in exchange for a chance at a billion-to-one possibility that they'll scoop the jackpot and be able to tell their boss to stuff it. The odd thing is, most lottery winners *don't* tell their bosses what they think of them and their crummy job. Most Canadians ACTUALLY STAY IN THEIR CRUMMY JOBS!

"Yeah, I just won $1.7 million, but I think I'll hang on to my job cleaning out septic tanks."

Lotteries were first started in Canada after the Olympics in Montreal, to help pay off the enormous debt left behind. It wasn't long (maybe a day or two) before the Feds realized they were onto something way better than taxes. Not only do lotteries bring in huge sums of cash, but Canadians actually *enjoy* handing over the dough!

PLAYING THE 6/49

Pick any six numbers, from one to forty-nine. Try this handy formula:

8: The number of days it takes Canada Post to deliver a letter mailed to an address across town.

36: How many times in the last week you've said the cable company is ripping you off and you're going to cancel their crummy service.

7: How many litres of booze you failed to declare at the border last time you came back from the U.S.

2,679: The number of lies told in the last election campaign. (*Doesn't count*, ed.)

12: How many weekends it rained last summer.

48: How many people told you to "Have a nice day," although in actual fact, they didn't really give a rat's ass whether you lived to see sundown.

23: The number of dollars you spent on Lotto 6/49 tickets last month, without winning a goddamn thing.

If this combination of numbers should win you $6 million, please send a cheque or money order for half the amount to:

Adrian Raeside
c/o Doubleday Canada
105 Bond Street
Toronto, Ontario
M5B 1Y3

NOTE: Please mark the envelope PERSONAL & CONFIDENTIAL, as
I don't trust those thieves at Doubleday....

The Military

THERE'S NO LIFE LIKE IT. (Especially if you're handy with a wrench and have a passion for antiques.)

For years, since the unification of the armed forces under the Pearson government, the Canadian forces have been suffering from a visibility problem. "No one seemed to know we existed," complained an air-force public affairs officer. This could be attributed to unification: the creation of one central public affairs office to inform the public of the latest military triumphs. The only triumphs in those dark days of neglect were the incredible engineering feats that took place in the military maintenance depots in the losing battle to keep antique and decrepit equipment running. To walk into a maintenance depot in the early 80s was (and in some cases still is) like walking into a mausoleum. One feels one should speak in hushed tones out of respect for the elderly and soon-to-be-departed.

The Tory administration finally reversed the slide, by de-unifying and issuing smart new kits to replace the universal puke green rags that had masqueraded as uniforms for so many years.

In addition, the navy were given new frigates, the air force got the CF-18 and the army? Uh, they got to go overseas to some festering, fly-blown country and mediate sordid civil wars.

CANADA'S NAVY

You notice the change as soon as you board one of Canada's new frigates. The crew are grinning like Cheshire cats, bursting to show you all the shiny new equipment that replaced the crap that was left over from the War of 1812. Deck plates aren't buckled, corridors are wide, wardrooms spacious, engine rooms are clean and bright, and the engines (gasp) actually work (sometimes). All revolutionary stuff. Canada's navy has finally broken free from the age of sail.

The ships aren't even called ships anymore. They're now called "defensive platforms"–although defence is no longer such a priority. External Affairs routinely commandeers a ship to show off Canada's industrial prowess. On these trips, the vessels become cocktail and canapé platforms, with the flight deck tarted up with displays and the Sea King helicopter serving as an antique punchbowl. "The display of sealskin lingerie? Yes sir, straight along the deck and it's to the left of the 57-millimetre cannon. Can't miss it."

Still, it's probably less dangerous than patrolling for Russian subs. No indications yet from Ottawa as to whether cirrhosis of the liver will be reclassed as a battlefield injury.

With the new ships comes pride. Maybe even vitality.
And who doesn't like playing with a new toy?

THE SUBMARINERS

Psst! wanna know a secret? Canada has submarines! No kidding.
Three of them. The *Onandaga*, the *Ojibwa* and the *Okanagan*. They
really belong in a museum, but heck, they run pretty well and it's
comforting to know that if there is a thermonuclear war, there will be
at least two-hundred-odd Canadians left to rebuild
Canada. (One can only hope that next time 'round
they don't bother about the Senate.)

Seriously, our subs are the *real* thing. Just like
in the movie *Das Boot* (and close to the same vintage).

Our subs aren't like the giant U.S. Trident submarines, nuclear missile–carrying, floating football
fields that our neighbours to the South slink
around in. Nah, we have tiny, smelly, cramped and
noisy underwater tramp steamers.

But they're ours.

Submariners are totally different from the sailors who serve on surface ships. Sub guys live in impossibly cramped quarters. (The two toilets are so small that the sailors have to remove their pants before shoe-horning themselves in.)

Submariners even have their own language:

"Skimmers": The Surface Navy

"Targets": Surface Navy Ships

"Sput": Surface Puke Under Training (new submariner)

There really is no life like it.

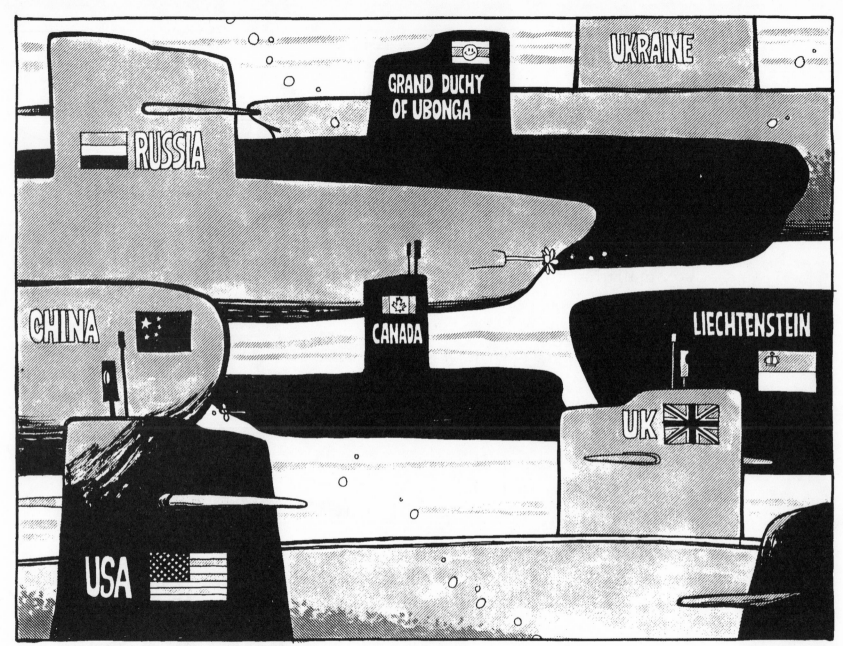

Meanwhile, under Canada's Arctic ice cap…

THE AIR FORCE

Like other branches of the forces, the Canadian air force's identity has been dusted off and is now proudly displayed. The air force also has new equipment, in the form of the CF–18 fighter, but a majority of their planes are older than the pilots who fly them. It's a classic Catch-22. If the pilots who fly the planes and the mechanics who service these antiques weren't so damn good, the federal government would have long ago been forced to replace these relics. It won't be long before they'll need archaeologists, not mechanics to fix these planes. One by one the old clunkers go out to pasture, stretching an already thin fleet. As it is, there are only enough aircraft for one contingent on peacekeeping duty, one on defence of the country and one in the shop.

ON BOARD A BUFFALO S&R AIRCRAFT

Able to stay up in the air for over eight hours at a stretch, these bright yellow planes feel heavy and slow. That's because they *are* heavy and slow. In the entire world, only six of these aircraft are still flying and guess what? They're in Canada. Used primarily for looking for lost boaters and idiot hikers, the Buffalo is extremely manoeuvrable and really quite roomy. Kind of like a high-tech cow barn—without the cows. For one who is used to dire warnings from the crew of commercial airliners as to what will happen if you even think of uncrossing your legs during takeoff and landing, it is a surprise to see the crew casually strolling about the cabin with coffee in hand two minutes after takeoff and during a 90-degree turn. A couple of unnecessary flights home by a couple of over-weight cabinet ministers burn up more fuel than it would take to outfit the entire Buffalo fleet.

We should make those MPs walk.

SEA KING HELICOPTERS

During the 1993 federal election, the then governing Tories had ordered the replacement EH101 helicopters from Europe. There was a terrible wailing and gnashing of teeth from the Liberal opposition when the cost of these new machines was revealed. There was nothing wrong with the Sea Kings they said. Jean Chrétien rode into the election using the cost of the EH101 helicopter as a broadsword, laying waste to the fiscally irresponsible Tory hun. If any of the cadre of lawyers and used car salesmen that made up the Liberal team had actually *flown* in one of the ancient Sea Kings, they may have changed their minds. (The closest any of the Liberal cabinet will come to something ancient in the air is downing a 1978 Bordeaux in Air Canada First Class.)

In peacetime, the biggest threat to these aircraft, besides government bean counters and engine failure, is the threat of large birds flying through the windshield. (Forget fixing the landing gear. Maybe a microwave oven might be more useful....)

The best view in the world has to be dangling your feet off the edge of the helicopter with the cargo door open, watching the world drift by. If this was part of the armed forces recruitment process, the recruiting offices would be mobbed with applicants. (Not recommended for anyone with vertigo.)

Returning to the base with a strong smell of fuel leaking into the cabin, I asked the pilot, Major Bob Henderson, if these helicopters are safe to fly. "Of course they are," he replied. "We wouldn't go up in them if they weren't."

Nine days later, Major Henderson was killed when his Sea King helicopter caught fire and crashed in New Brunswick.

THE SNOWBIRDS

You've seen them at airshows, you've watched them perform impossible loops and rolls, all at over two-hundred kilometres an hour and in perfect formation. The Snowbirds are about the only Canadian icon that will make Canadians stop and pay attention.

My invitation to fly with the Snowbirds was one I couldn't– and didn't–pass up.

It can take a couple of hours to prepare for a Snowbird flight. First, a medical exam from the base doctor to make sure you have a pulse and won't have to be pried out of the cockpit as a corpse.

Next, your flight suit. A warning for the fashion conscious: they only come in one colour. Blue. At the very best, you'll look like Mr. Goodwrench.

Next, get fitted for a helmet. All the Snowbird helmets are moulded to individual pilots' heads, so don't expect a perfect fit. Mine felt like a 500lb vise.

Next, a parachute and inflatable life vest. The parachute feels damn heavy. By this point, you weigh an extra twenty kilos and look like you belong on the set of the movie *Plan 9 From Outer Space*.

Finally, you're fitted for an oxygen mask and given explicit instructions on how to use the ejection seat and parachute. The briefing is anything *but* brief and is very complicated. I lose interest. Let's face it. If there *is* an emergency, I'm pulling every lever within reach and getting the hell outta there. (Or, I'll stay with the plane and someone cashes in my life insurance policy.)

Yesss. The time has come. I'm strapped into the plane by a flight engineer. In a matter of minutes, the Snowbirds taxi down the runway, including Snowbird #7, containing yours truly, wetting himself from anticipation. Takeoff is in groups of three and is surprisingly quick and smooth.

The Snowbirds quickly get into formation. By formation, I really mean formation. There are only two-and-a-half feet separating two planes' wingtips. All the pilots follow radio instructions from their leader, Snowbird #1. My pilot, Steve, flew the whole time with his head turned, watching the plane next to us on the right. That plane flew watching the plane on his right and in turn, that plane watches Snowbird #1. This is all at over two-hundred kilometres an hour.

After flying for about thirty-five minutes, zooming through the mountain ranges in formation, brilliant blue sky above and sparkling snowfields below, I asked Steve, "They actually *pay* you for doing this?"

Our first loop. We suddenly find ourselves flying vertically. The G-forces push me back on the seat. I feel the blood draining from my head. I'm crushed back in my seat. I can barely lift my hands

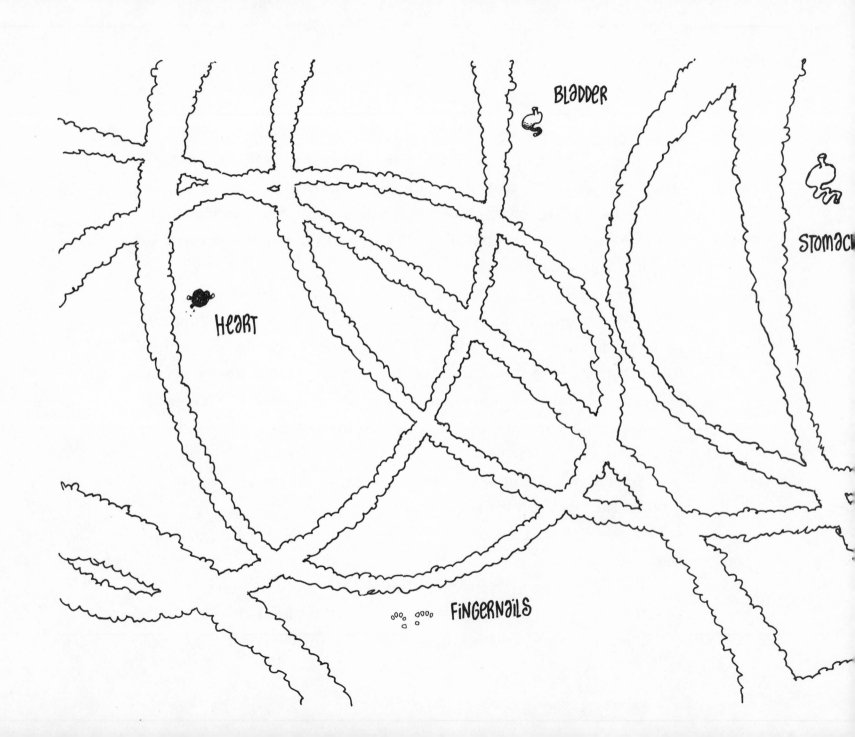

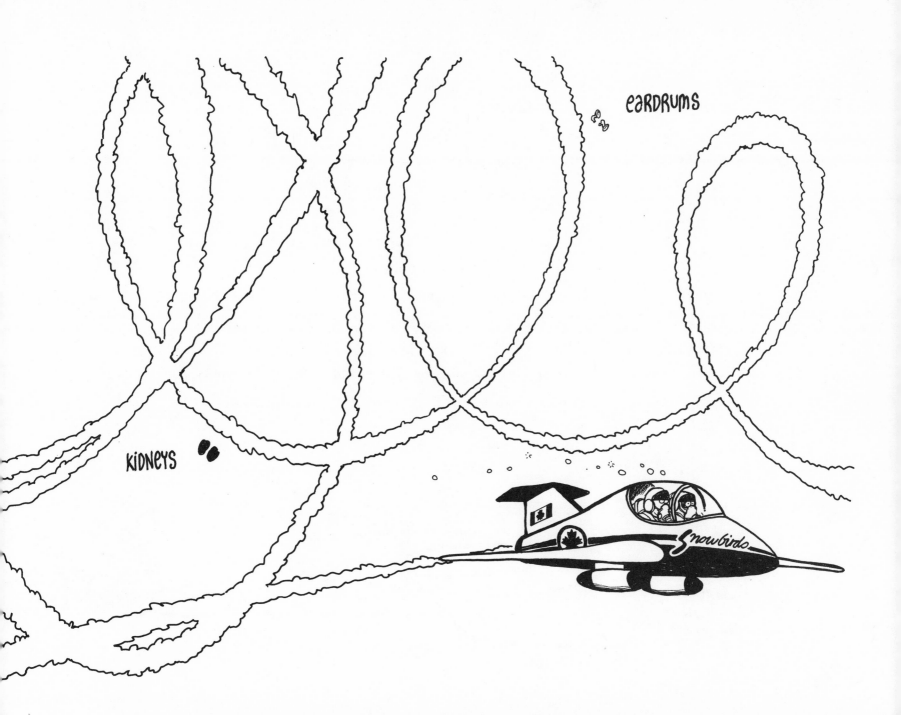

from my lap. Although the jet's engines are going full throttle, all I can hear is the pilot gasping for air as the G-forces rearrange his lungs.

Suddenly, all is quiet as we reach the top of the loop and lie on our backs for a few seconds. On the downward side, the ground rushes up to meet us. We pull out at what seems like the last second and once again, the G-forces redistribute my insides. I turned to Steve and said, "Whatever they're paying you, it isn't enough."

If the air force should ever charge the public admission for one-hour Snowbird trips, we could probably retire our national deficit in two years. Or less.

Politics

How could King John have known, when he put his X on the Magna Carta at Runnymede in 1215 to rid the country of dictatorship, corruption, abuse of power and patronage, that in Canada, some 700-odd years later, would emerge a virtual dictatorship riddled with corruption, abuses of power and patronage. What started out as a pretty good system, based on individual representation and large numbers of small parties forming loose coalitions, has been twisted and mutated into what we have today, one party with the majority of seats in a house where 51 per cent of the vote carries the day. The opposition parties can rant and rave all they want but it is just for show. Unless a third of the government members call in sick, or are vacationing in Florida at the time of a vote, the government gets its way.

Canada's Political System:

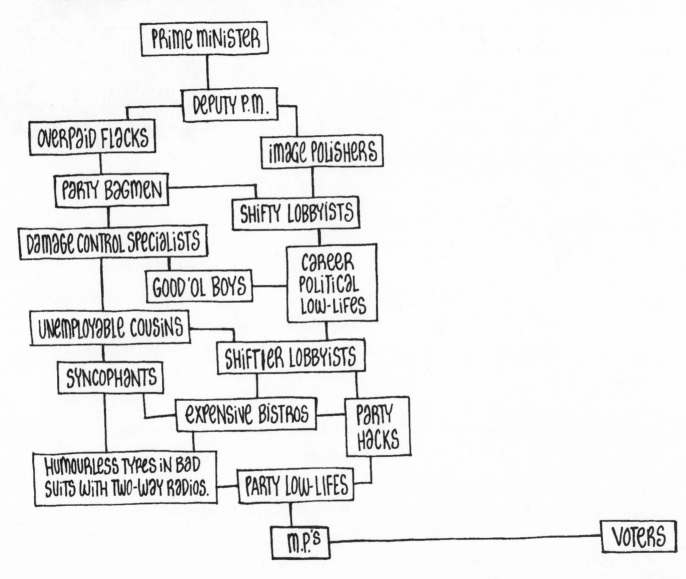

GLOSSARY OF POLITICAL TERMS:

NON-CONFIDENCE VOTE:

When the opposition members put aside their dislike of each other long enough to call for a vote of non-confidence on a government action. Usually held when as many members are away as possible.

DIVISION BELLS:

These are rung throughout the parliament building to signal an upcoming vote in the Commons. The real idea is to wake MPs dozing over travel brochures, or warn those in the parliamentary dining room they only have time for one more shrimp cocktail.

CAUCUS:

When all the members of a party meet behind closed doors to discuss political strategy. Usually just a get-together to discuss the previous night's cocktail crawl or upcoming holiday travel, er, fact-finding mission.

RESEARCHERS:

Skilled personnel attached to every official party (*surely NOT the Tories,* ed.) to assist MPs in formulating policy and strategy. Usually the cousin of a member, or an unemployable campaign worker.

THE NOT-SO-GREAT PURSUIT

Canadian elections are all about masochism. You gotta be a masochist to run and you gotta be a masochist to follow one. There are always the political junkies, journalists, cartoonists, political science professors and other losers who actually enjoy this process of elimination (or are paid to cover it, ahem) but for most Canadians elections are exercises in futility. Not only does an election cost us enormous amounts of money, every election since the last one Sir John A. Macdonald belched his way through has only served to reinforce to Canadians what total idiots all politicians are. Every time out we get a candidate who says he/she is different form the others and is a crusader to change the system. This is complete and utter bull. Those swine will tell you anything to get elected. If the polls tell them that the majority of Canadians want their next prime minister to be an Elvis impersonator, then, like magic, your candidate will campaign tirelessly wearing sideburns and a large white jumpsuit. In Canadian politics, if you can fake sincerity, you've got it made.

THE MAGIC OF POLITICS:

Meet Clem. Clem was gettin' tired of bein' surrounded by mindless, overweight hawgs.

So Clem ran for public office. He made some speeches, ate some BBQ chicken...

Next thing yer know, ol' Clem was elected and on his way to Ottawa...

OTTWA

And once again, Clem is surrounded by mindless, overweight hawgs...

The Following is a List of Promises that Must be Made to Guarantee a Seat in the House of Commons:

- Abolish the Senate.

- Tattoo American flags on senators' butts and parachute them into Teheran during flog-an-American-month.

- Turn the senate chamber into a casino.

- Turn the Commons into a bingo hall.

- Sponsor an annual flog-an-economist day.

- Appoint a homeless person as the Minister of Housing.

- Allow the bars in Ottawa to stay open until 4 a.m. (Our elected reps will be too hung over to do any further damage.)

- Declare open season on lobbyists. (Preferably during their rutting season, October 1–September 30.)

- Hold a swap-meet at the National Gallery and try to trade "Voice of Fire" for something tasteful in black velvet.

Like it or not, it's the media that have a large part in deciding the out-
come of any election. A hundred years ago, most Canadians had no
idea who their MP was, nor had they ever met him/her. (More likely
him in those unenlightened days.) With television news now broad-
cast live, twenty-four hours a day, we have the thrill of seeing
extreme close-ups of our poxy, sclerotic, liver-spotted candidates for
the hallowed chamber live and in our livingrooms.

We are a nation that sits in front of our TVs and decides the
next prime minister solely on what can be jammed in between a clip
on the latest cellulite reduction cream and a hemorrhoids commercial. How appropriate.

To experience an election campaign the way it used to be, go to
a local all-candidates meeting. Chances are, the only media there will
be a reporter from the local newspaper and someone from the local
cable TV company.

All-candidates meetings are usually held in small halls or
school gymnasiums. Each candidate is given a few minutes to make
an opening statement. Usually the same old rubbish promising jobs,
prosperity, honest open government, change, argle bargle.... The

voters who turned out for these forums aren't interested in hearing that. They're already jockeying for a position at the free microphone(s), clutching dog-eared scraps of paper, or terrifyingly thick files, all with specific questions for one or all of the candidates. Some of these Qs are "softies" designed to make the candidate of their choice look good, i.e:

This question direction to the Reform candidate: "Sir, does your party have any plans to bring down the massive deficit left to us by those dishonest Tory scum?"

Candidate responds: "Why, thank you for bringing up that important issue. As a matter of fact, we have a comprehensive plan that came to our illustrious leader the archangel Preston Manning in a vision he had while slopping out the pigs at his hog farm in High River. This fascinating 100,000 point plan is..." You get the picture.

There are the other questions, with the inevitable one that no one can answer, but to which all the candidates must listen politely and try to look half intelligent:

This question to all candidates: "What do you plan to do about the misuse of the electromagnetic spectrum by the alien civilization from the Sprag Galaxy that has set up in Terrace Bay, Ontario? I have supporting evidence here (pauses to brandish file full of newspaper clippings and notepaper covered in crabbed scribbles in crayon) that there is a plot to infiltrate and eventually disrupt all electronic communications, eventually bringing society and re-runs of Lawrence Welk to a halt."

Then there is the delicious no-win question every candidate dreads: This question to the Progressive Conservative candidate (when there *was* a PC party): "How do you justify the huge profits now being reaped by the drug companies now that patents are extended on their drugs, allowing them to artificially keep the price of medication beyond the reach of most pensioners?"

The other candidates will all grin like Cheshire cats and turn to watch the PC candidate mess his pants while slowly sinking in his seat. There is a horrible fascination in watching someone commit suicide right in front of you. The PC candidate is later spotted running into a one-hour cleaners.

THE FOLLOWING IS A SAMPLE QUESTION AS ANSWERED BY ALL THE CANDIDATES IN 1993'S FEDERAL ELECTION:

What plan do you or your party have for economic prosperity?

LIBERAL: "As you will read in the Liberal Party's Red Book, I have a copy right here, pages 23 to 24 outline the precious thoughts of our formidable leader Jean Chrétien, who has put together a comprehensive prosperity plan that is so brilliant it had to be preserved forever in this magnificent book free for anyone phoning 1–800–SHA–FTME. There you will see on pages, uh, 19 to 21 exactly why a Liberal vote on the 25th is a vote for housing, jobs, a second motorhome..."

TORY: "If anybody had been listening to *us* over the last eight years, and not those biased scum–sucking pigs in the media, you would realize just what a sterling job we have been doing keeping this country on its knees, er, feet. Oh sure, a third of our caucus was investigated by the RCMP, our previous leader was a thief, we gave the country to the Americans and taxed you into extinction. But, hey, we're different now, we've got a new leader, new faces in cabinet. Let us go back and show you that we can finish you off..uh, finish this job off.

NDP: "You should count your blessings you live in this great country of ours. Things are great, we have medicare, jobs, Anne Murray, wow! This is the place to live, all because of our voice of social conscience in the Commons. O.K. O.K. we have no real party leader, but that doesn't matter, it's the NDP philosophy that will pull us through these dark times ahead. We've got a plan for economic prosperity, but no one is listening to us anyway, so why bother wasting our breath. Oh God, what am I doing here?"

REFORM: "The first thing we'll do is get rid of anyone who isn't white, who hasn't done their military service and who speaks like a hillbilly. Bring back hanging for stealing a loaf of bread, put single moms to work in the asbestos mines, abolish health care for those making more than a military pension, why, I remember a time when we were pinned down by Chinese on Hill 281 in Korea, we had only two bullets left, but we had the conviction that what we were doing was right. Well, we somehow pulled through, and by God we'll do it again! If not for Preston Manning's dogged determination when he was wandering in the wilderness for the last few years, and listening to the grassroots, I wouldn't be here today. The all-being saviour will be at the local soccer stadium this Sunday at twelve noon. Donations gratefully received."

NATURAL LAW PARTY: "The first thing we will do is hire ten-thousand yogic flyers (an air traffic controller's nightmare) and over-whelm our economic problems by harmonic osmosis. The Natural Law's platform was based on the power of collective thought ridding us of evil. We all know that doesn't work, as most senators are still pulling a paycheque."

INDEPENDENT: "It's time to give the people more say in government decisions. We will have faxes in every house, robotized cars, robot-ized toilets. The future is in communications. We shouldn't be send-ing our natural resources away; let us manufacture robots right here."

Great stuff. But like all elections, come voting day, Canadians held their noses, closed their eyes and voted for the least obnoxious.

How to Spot the Players on Parliament Hill:

THE LIBERALS

Supremely confident with a cocky stride. Wear nicely-tailored suits and carry cell phones so they can be in constant contact with lobbyists.

THE TORIES

Although they are not officially supposed to be there, they lurk in the basement of the parliament buildings like lepers, looking for political scraps and any sign of redemption.

THE REFORM PARTY

Still fighting the Boer War, reformers are the Branch Davidians of Canadian politics. A good way to spot a reformer at an Ottawa cocktail party is to holler out "Preston's a pussy."

THE NDP

Sad individuals in badly–fitting tweed. They're like those bums you see on Broadway: "He coulda been a star, y'know, but he blew it . . ."

THE BLOC

Sad individuals in badly–fitting cotton. They're like those bums you see on Broadway: "He coulda been a star, y'know, but he blew it . . ."

The Post Office:

CANADA'S LARGEST SHELTERED
WORKSHOP

Without the unique activities (*inactivities, surely*, ed.) of Canada Post, fax machines would still barely rate a paragraph in *Popular Mechanics* and couriers would still deliver telegrams.

Canada Post has done more to advance high-tech alternate communications than NASA has in the last 20 years. Canadians turned to faxes and couriers because posting an important letter or package and expecting it to get to its destination across town in less than a week, was a leap of faith of the same magnitude as expecting the Virgin Mary to turn up at 6.30 p.m. and give you a hot-oil massage.

Canada Post has also brought Canadians together, united under one common cause. *Everybody* has a Canada Post horror story.

CANADA POST CHUCKLES

 Letter to a very alive recipient returned, marked "deceased."

 Correctly addressed letter to a P.O. Box returned, marked, "addressee unknown."

 Package weighed and paid for at the counter, returned a week later for .20¢ insufficient postage.

 Counter clerk asleep at his wicket.

The blame for this appalling service is usually directed toward "the system," when, in actual fact, it should be directed toward the cretins who work in the post office. You would think that if you were getting paid more per hour than the average brain surgeon, you'd put just a tiny bit of pride or effort into your job....

Canada Post, in an effort to lure Canadians back to the fold, has set up retail outlets in malls and convenience stores. Looks great from the outside–staff who care, quick service. The only flaw in the system, is whatever you post leaves this oasis of quality and ends up languishing in a Canada Post sorting depot outside Dorval.

On the upside, if you suffer from lethargy or high blood pressure, just pop down to your local unionized post office.

It's a fabulous tonic.

Sporting Life

"I went to a fight the other night and a hockey game broke out."

That line has been around as long as there has been hockey, and it's not far from the truth. Hockey has become one big free-for-all. Sometimes, it's difficult to remember that the players are all highly-skilled professionals, skating at the very edge of their abilities, with one goal in mind–winning the illustrious Stanley Cup (with a few product endorsements thrown in along the way).

Watching a hockey game on TV isn't the same as actually *being* at the arena. A hockey game is so fast that if you briefly divert your attention to the crazed fan waving a four-foot-high sign reading "Gretzky's a sissy," two goals and three fights might have already occurred.

MEET STAN:

STAN IS AN ACCOUNTANT. STAN HAS NEVER RAISED HIS VOICE IN ANGER.

IN FACT STAN GETS ALONG WITH ABSOLUTELY EVERYONE.

THAT'S A LOVELY STAPLER, MRS. CLEAVER.

BUT WHEN STAN GOES DOWN TO THE HOCKEY ARENA,

STAN GOES THROUGH A REMARKABLE TRANSFORMATION:

SWING THAT STICK HARDER! YOU BUM! C'MON YOU PUSSIES, HIT HIT!

The fans are more fun than the players. Audience participation is part of the "ambience" of a hockey game. Impossible costumes will appear, language will become "creative" and signs proclaiming everything from "Don Cherry is God," to "Wendell Clark's a girl" are displayed.

With the price of admission also comes the fans' right to question every referee call:

"WHATTAYERMEAN IT'S NOT A GOAL?! IT WENT INTO THE NET YOU BLIND MORON!" "THAT WASN'T A PENALTY! GET GLASSES, ____HOLE!"

Not exactly an evening at the opera, but lots more fun. Besides, where else can a Canadian let loose and break the unwritten code of carefully-crafted civility?

   Not only is hockey fun. You can make money off it too. Even though the average office hockey pool is more complicated than a trigonometry textbook, even the most cretinous sports fan can be Einstein once the hockey pool is posted. As the teams advance to the playoffs and a possible Stanley Cup victory, the money and excite-ment mount to a fever pitch. In fact, all office conversation not relat-ed to hockey ceases. If the U.S. were ever to invade Canada, all they'd have to do is wait until the evening of the final game of the Stanley Cup and they could drive their tanks right up Yonge Street unopposed and unnoticed.

   (God help them, however, if Canada should lose again to the New York Rangers. The invaders would be mercilessly slaughtered.)

BASEBALL

Baseball is sacred to our American cousins. *They* invented it (they say), *they* perfected it and only *they* know how to play it. But then the Toronto Blue Jays won the World Series – twice in a row. We humiliated an entire country just by hitting a small white ball farther and more often than the Americans did.

But hitting the ball is not all there is to baseball. Baseball is a huge machine made up of managers, agents, talent scouts, investors, bankers and stockbrokers. There is big money to be made at the diamond. (Surely enough to purchase an entire diamond mine.) Some players get paid more than the GNP of most African countries. All this for standing around for most of a given game, spitting tobacco. (Why is it the camera always does a close-up on a player just when he lets loose with a stream of foul brown liquid?) With all the money those pro ball players make, why can't they chew (and swallow) caviar instead?

At one time, every Canadian boy would dream of being a hockey player in the NHL and would spend hours on frozen ponds, practicing their stickhandling. Nowadays, good Canadian lads are much more savvy, and each dreams of being a baseball player. At least the equipment isn't as expensive and their parents don't need to get up at 3 a.m. to drive them to the only arena that has available icetime.

Baseball is probably the only business in Canada (besides hockey) where it doesn't matter what outrageous admission prices you charge – fans will always flock to see their team. Heck, they'll even buy seasons' tickets months before they know if their team is going to stink this year or not. At least, unlike hockey, most baseball games are played outdoors (unless Toronto's Skydome roof fails to retract – again) and what better way to spend a Friday afternoon out of the office? "I'd love to go over the Herfinger account with you, but I'm getting a root canal this afternoon." Or alternately, if your team is last in the standings: "I'd love to go to the game with you, but I'm getting a root canal this afternoon."

What a baseball player does on his time off:

10:50	Wake up, chew tobacco
10:52	Spit tobacco
11:00	Phone stockbroker
11:15	Phone accountant, chew tobacco
11:30	Spit tobacco
11:35	Phone currency trader
12:00	Lunch with banker
12:15	Spit tobacco on banker
1:30	Check out new Ferraris
1:35	Buy one, chew tobacco
1:37	Spit tobacco on seat
2:30	Meeting with agent
3:45	Photo shoot endorsing product he's never heard of
4:00	Spit tobacco
4:15	Nap

Stepping Out

For some bizarre reason, Canadians have a reputation for being quiet and somewhat introverted.

But just stand inside any medium-sized Canadian bar on a Friday night and you'd really have to stretch your imagination to picture the patrons sitting quietly, reading Pierre Berton books.

In the past, Canadian pubs were also known as Beer Parlours, perhaps in an effort to conceal from our lingering Victorian sensibilities what really goes on in a pub.

Things have changed. Provincial drinking laws are more relaxed and neighbourhood pubs and brew pubs have sprung up in residential areas. Some of these are theme pubs as in "The Jolly Chamberpot

English Pubbe," "The Loyalist Redcoat Arms," and "The Arr Matey Waterfront Tavern."

The only province that has remained above it all is Quebec, where the bistros and cafés have always served anything, anywhere, anytime and to whoever they damn well please. A most civilized place.

Like other countries, Canada has had its problems with alcohol abuse. Small, isolated Northern communities, like Davis Inlet in Labrador, are drowning in a sea of whiskey and gasoline fumes. The young are hit the hardest, as depression, abuse, and unemployment compound into a hopelessness that can only be forgotten inside a garbage bag filled with gas. The government's solution has been to lock up those found wandering the snowbanks in an unleaded daze. (Fewer taxes on gas than on whiskey?)

Put yourself in the Northern Natives' position. If you and your family were moved into a one-room shack in a barren area hundreds of miles from a supermarket, school or hospital and the plane fare to civilization cost more than you make on welfare in three months, you might have your head in a bag of gas, too.

When was the last time you saw a full-page ad from a wealthy, overbureaucratized Canadian charity soliciting money for Davis Inlet and other impoverished Northern communities?... Just asking.

HOUSE PARTIES

Soirées du Maison vary depending on geographic location.

In uptight Toronto, unless you know the hosts very well, you're not likely to be invited to someone's house. More likely, you'll all meet in a bar or restaurant. This eliminates the problem of finding excuses to fling the guests out of the house when they get boring or they start wrecking the house.

In the Maritimes, getting an invitation to someone's house is as simple as making eye contact. Maritimers are (in)famous for their hospitality and think nothing of inviting a total stranger into their house. (These days, with nearly the entire fishery wiped out, the rum flows a little less freely.)

Quebecers tend to congregate in bars and bistros. With liberal closing times, fabulous food and great wine, why not? Besides, after 1 a.m., these establishments tend to take on the atmosphere of your own livingroom anyway.

The vastness of the prairies makes visiting difficult, as do the harsh winters. But for those hardy Canadians, curling, skating and bingo act as social diversions. Relatives tend to visit often, but those who are friends and neighbours are too damn busy scratching out a living in the summer to socialize much.

In British Columbia, a house party usually gets as far as the deck. Any excuse for a barbecue. Vancouverites take it to the extreme. Barbecues can be spotted on balconies and decks regardless of the weather. A lot of these hard-core wintertime barbecuers are newly-converted arrived refugees from central Canada, who are enduring just so they can phone Uncle Al in Hamilton in February and gloat, "Al, you'll never believe what we did yesterday...."

Picnics are big on the West coast, with each pic-nicker trying to outdo the other when it comes to what they have in their baskets. "Oh fabulous, dogwood leaves stuffed with sliced gnu livers and caviar. Did you get the caviar from the bulk food section?" Pretentious picnics are big in Lotus Land.

BLOODY CAESAR

1-1/2 oz vodka
3 oz clamato juice
1 tsp lemon juice
several drops Worcestershire sauce
several drops Tabasco sauce

Combine with ice; shake well. Strain and serve
straight up. Add salt and pepper to taste.
Garnish with celery stalk, if desired.

Apparently, the Bloody Caesar cocktail was invented in Alberta. This all-Canadian concoction contains only a modicum of alcohol, lots of healthy clam and tomato juice and is garnished with the most civilized and least offensive of all vegetables – celery. The result is a cocktail that is actually *good* for you. Even the politically correct can find no fault with it. Unless you belong to the KSPCRC (Kingston Society for the Prevention of Cruelty to Razor Clams).

DINING OUT

Food.   One thing that Canada has an abundance of.
Unfortunately, thanks to the Trans-Canada highway and the fast
food chain stores, many of Canada's culinary treats are exactly the
same.   These companies spend millions developing hamburgers
and buns that taste just like a hunk of cardboard between two

slices of dishcloth. And whether you eat cardboard in Halifax or Victoria, IT IS GUARANTEED TO TASTE EXACTLY THE SAME! If you really want nutritional value, you're better off tossing away the hamburger and eating the box it came in.

And if the smell of rancid grease and molded plastic tables doesn't cut it with you, take heart. Canada is loaded with smaller, independently-owned restaurants serving good local food. If you're used to American portions, forget it. Canadians are far more petite when they eat. The only thing big in Canadian restaurants is the bill.

What To Eat in Canada

MARITIMES: Lobster. Lobster and butter, lobster boiled, lobster steamed, cold lobster, cold lobster in a bun. Hell, you can even get McLobster burgers.

OTTAWA: There is nothing to eat in Ottawa. Go to Hull.

MONTREAL: Any possible type of food at prices from the ridiculous to the ridiculous. If it is cooked in the province of Quebec it is delicious. If Quebec ever separates, Canada will become a gastronomic wasteland or die of malnutrition.

Eating in Quebec is an event. Unlike in Toronto, where after you've finished your meal, the waiter will hover around your table like Marley's ghost, waiting to clear the table for the next customer. Take your time in Montreal. Settle in for the evening. That is your table and you are encouraged to stay as long as you damn well please.

TORONTO: This is a city that has just emerged from the dark ages of liquor licensing. The city fathers are still terrified that someone might have a good time in a bar or restaurant.

VANCOUVER: Vancouver emerged from its gastronomic shell after Expo '86 when the Asian invasion began. Hong Kong Chinese, Taiwanese and Japanese flooded the city. The Chinese and Taiwanese immigrated (legally, or otherwise)–the Japanese were just shopping. There's now at least one sushi bar and three Chinese restaurants per block in Vancouver.

How is it that every roadside café in Canada offers something "homemade"? Do the "homemade" fries *really* come from home? Is there really someone who nips home every noon hour, cooks up a batch of raspberry jam, then carefully fills those little plastic containers you find on every café table? Just asking.

TAKE ME DOWN TO THE BLACKFLY FESTIVAL

Americans love to park themselves at baseball diamonds every summer. This pastime provides a meeting place for friends and family.

Canadians love to go to festivals. Festivals are held continually, so it seems, in every small and not-so-small town across Canada. The theme of the festival generally depends on the location.

As far as I know, Ottawa hasn't held a "Festival of Excess"–yet.

The Sooke Canoe Race 'n Pancake-Eating,
Axe-Throwing Competition

The Antigonish Tattoo

sex in canada:

The Underground Economy

THE LAND THE GST FORGOT

Forget going to the shopping malls. Drive down any secondary road in any province and you can probably buy everything you need, as well as a lot of things you *don't* need. But these merchants go by the old saying, "There is someone for everything." You bet. There *has* to be someone who wants a wooden wheelbarrow planter, a wooden wheelbarrow planter pushed by a wooden gnome, or a wooden wheelbarrow planter pushed by a wooden Elvis gnome or a dazzling array of freshly-killed chickens/lamb/rabbit/ducks and other unfortunate farm animals. The beauty is that it is all ABSOLUTELY TAX FREE. Unless these people confess under threat of torture (watching "Question Period" for twelve hours) the federal government will know nothing about these transactions. Besides,

policing it would take the entire staff at Revenue Canada and the resources of the Canadian military, including air strikes, just to track down 1 per cent of our thriving underground economy.

OUR THRIVING UNDERGROUND ECONOMY

The Feds do nothing short of helping to unload the boats when it comes to cigarette smuggling. They like to blame it on the Natives, but despite a brief period at Oka, Canada's aboriginal population is not known for their organizational skills. It's the white guys who are profiting from the massive cigarette smuggling. Every night, from the St. Lawrence to the Gulf Islands, shadowy figures in boats and cars (sometimes semi trucks) shuttle back and forth with enough health-destroying cigs to wipe out a medium-sized town.

Not all Canadians participate in this jolly pastime of cheating Revenue Canada. Apart from the 90 per cent of travellers to the U.S. who conveniently "forget" to declare twocartonsofcigarettesacouple-oflitresofvodka2pairsofshoes5CDsacoupleofleatherjacketsandtwobag-sofgroceries, there are those who are scrupulously honest when it comes to declaring the plaster busts of Napoleon and other cultural gems acquired while abroad. You've seen them. They're the ones on airplanes who are poring over receipts for every souvenir ashtray and converting $1.98 (U.S.) into our worthless Canadian currency.

These people are not true Canadians and should have drinks spilled on them.

Weather (or not)

The electronic message boards in the Tokyo subways scroll the latest financial information. In U.S. subways, it's the latest sports scores. In Canadian subways, it's the weather.

God help the cable system that doesn't have the weather channel on basic cable. If it wasn't for the weather, we'd all be a race of mutes. The weather is the opening line for almost any telephone conversation:

"How's the weather?"
"Can you believe the weather?"
"The weather's been just crazy."
"If the weather doesn't improve, I'm going to go crazy."

"The weather's driving me crazy."
"Have you heard what the weather's doing for Saturday?"

Of course, if you live on the West coast and you are phoning central Canada anytime in February, the conversation would be a little different:

"You wouldn't *believe* the weather we've been having."
"The weather's been just *fabulous!*"
"If the weather doesn't break, we're gonna have another drought."
"I'm sorry to hear about *your* weather."

On the other hand, if you are phoning from central Canada in June, when the West coast is flopping about in its seasonal two feet of flood water, the conversation would be roughly the same.

THE WEATHER MAP OF CANADA:

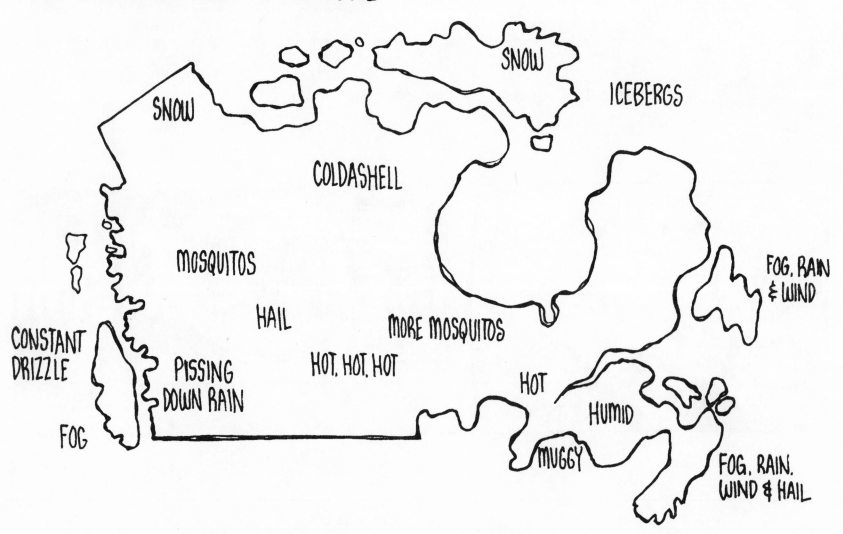

Zebra Mussels

Originally stow-aways on a freighter from Europe, Zebra Mussels have, in the last few years, made themselves quite at home in the Great Lakes. What was once a fascinating little critter for marine biologists to study has become a menace to anything that floats. Zebra Mussels cling to anything – hulls, pilings, ropes, water intakes, buoys, cross-channel swimmers…

Unfortunately, they are not edible and you cannot smoke them, so these pro wrestlers of the bi-valve family continue to bully their way across the waters of Canada.

Epilogue

O.K. so Canada has a few warts. The difference between us and the "other" guys is that our warts are kinder and gentler.

Being kinder and gentler also means we're an easy mark over at the U.N., who blithely order up squads of Canadian peacekeepers at the drop of a grenade. Canadians spend more time defending camels than we do polar bears.

Maybe that's what defines us.. We fall all over ourselves protecting the rights of others. We are certainly tolerant of the unique customs and peculiar habits of immigrants to this country. Deep down, all Canadians are aware that we are all newcomers to this country (except the Natives, who were, of course, here first) and we have only had a few hundred years to leave our imprint.

We're still wrestling with the idea that we REALLY do belong to this country. Remember, we're different from the United States and everyone else; we've got fresh water, Medicare, reasonably intact natural resources, talented people and air you can breathe.

Give Canada a big hug.